**Collins**

**KS2 M**

**Reasoning**

Reasoning

**SATs Question Book**

Age 10 – 11

Key Stage 2

SATs Question Book

Katherine Pate

# Contents

- You will need a pen, pencil, ruler, eraser and protractor.

- You may **not** use a calculator to answer any of the questions.

- Some questions have a method box. For these questions you get a mark for showing your method.

- Show your working out in the space provided or in the space around the question.

- There are three progress tests throughout the book to allow you to practise the skills again. Record your results in the progress charts to identify what you are doing well in and what you can improve.

**Acknowledgements**

Every effort has been made to trace copyright holders and obtain their permission for the use of copyright material. The author and publisher will gladly receive information enabling them to rectify any error or omission in subsequent editions. All facts are correct at time of going to press.

Images and illustrations are
© Shutterstock.com and
© HarperCollinsPublishers

Published by Collins
An imprint of HarperCollins*Publishers*
1 London Bridge Street,
London SE1 9GF

© HarperCollins*Publishers* Limited

ISBN 9780008201630

First published 2016

10 9 8 7 6 5 4 3

All rights reserved. No part of this publication may be reproduced, stored in a retrieval system, or transmitted, in any form or by any means, electronic, mechanical, photocopying, recording or otherwise, without the prior permission of Collins.

British Library Cataloguing in Publication Data.

A CIP record of this book is available from the British Library.

Commissioning Editor: Michelle l'Anson
Author: Katherine Pate
Project Management and Editorial: Louise Williams and Katie Galloway
Cover Design: Sarah Duxbury and Paul Oates
Inside Concept Design: Paul Oates and Ian Wrigley
Text Design and Layout: Contentra Technologies
Production: Lyndsey Rogers
Printed in Great Britain

# Place Value and Rounding

**1** Write 609 in words.

_____

1 mark

**2** Round **8,946**

to the nearest 10 [            ]

1 mark

to the nearest 100 [            ]

1 mark

to the nearest 1000 [            ]

1 mark

**3** Use each digit once to make:

[ 1 ]        [ 5 ]        [ 7 ]        [ 2 ]        [ 6 ]

the largest possible number _____

1 mark

the smallest possible number _____

1 mark

**4** Write the next three terms in this sequence:

6,632    6,732    6,832    [            ] ,    [            ] ,    [            ]

3 marks

# Place Value and Rounding

**5** Circle two numbers in the box that round to 15,000.

| 14,826 | | 14,400 |
|--------|--------|--------|
| | 15,917 | |
| 14,329 | | 15,415 |
| | 15,500 | |

2 marks

**6** Write the value of the 7 in 9,712,000.

_____

1 mark

**7** Here are the populations of some cities:

| City | Population |
|------|-----------|
| Madrid | 3,233,500 |
| London | 8,630,100 |
| Athens | 3,090,500 |
| Berlin | 3,520,000 |
| Paris | 2,241,000 |

Complete this list of cities in order of population size.

**1)** London  **2)** Berlin  **3)** _____  **4)** _____  **5)** _____

2 marks

**8** Complete:

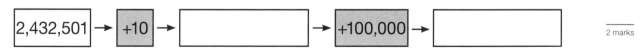

2,432,501 → +10 → [     ] → +100,000 → [     ]

2 marks

Total marks ............ /16        How am I doing?

5

# Negative Numbers

**1** Write the next three terms in this sequence:

3, 2, 1, 0, –1, _____, _____, _____

*3 marks*

**2** Write these numbers in order, starting with the largest:

1, –5, 2, 6, –2, 0

| | | | | | |
|---|---|---|---|---|---|
| | | | | | |

*3 marks*

**3** The table shows the temperatures in four towns one day.

| Aberdeen | –6°C |
|---|---|
| Cardiff | 3°C |
| London | –1°C |
| Belfast | 0°C |

**a)** Which city was coldest? _____

*1 mark*

**b)** Which city had the highest temperature? _____

*1 mark*

**4** The temperature in a freezer is –5°C.

Amy leaves the freezer door open.

The temperature goes up by 3°C.

What is the temperature of the freezer now?

_____

*1 mark*

# Negative Numbers

**5** Write the missing terms in this sequence:

____, –4, –1, ____, ____

**6** Work out the difference between –3°C and 5°C.

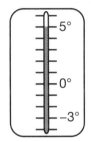

_____

1 mark

**7** The table shows the average winter and summer temperatures for three cities.

| City | Average summer temperature | Average winter temperature |
|---|---|---|
| Toronto | 26°C | –10°C |
| Moscow | 22°C | –13°C |
| Beijing | 25°C | –8°C |

**a)** Which city has the coldest winter temperature? _____

1 mark

**b)** Which city has the greatest difference between its summer and winter

temperatures? _____

1 mark

Total marks ............. /15          How am I doing?

# Roman Numerals

**1** Write the number shown below.

XXIV

[          ]

1 mark

**2** Write the time shown on this clock:

[          ] minutes past [          ]

1 mark

**3** Here are some years written in Roman numerals.

[   ] MDCCIV     [   ] MMLIX     [   ] MCMLV     [   ] MMIX     [   ] MMIV

**a)** Tick 2009

1 mark

**b)** Write the dates in order, starting with the earliest.

[          ]  [          ]  [          ]  [          ]  [          ]

2 marks

Total marks ............. /5          How am I doing?

8

# All Kinds of Numbers

**1** Complete these factor pairs of 12:

$1 \times \boxed{\phantom{00}}$     $\boxed{\phantom{00}} \times 6$     $3 \times \boxed{\phantom{00}}$

*3 marks*

**2**  **a)** Write all the factors of 20 in this box.

$\boxed{\phantom{xxxxxxxxxxxxxxxxxxxxxxx}}$

*2 marks*

**b)** Write all the prime factors of 20 in this box.

$\boxed{\phantom{xxxxxxxxxxxxxxxxxxxxxxx}}$

*1 mark*

**3** A perfect number is the sum of its factors, except itself.
28 is a perfect number because:

The factors of 28 are     1, 2, 4, 7, 14, 28

and     $1 + 2 + 4 + 7 + 14 = 28$

Show that 6 is a perfect number.

The factors of 6 are     _____

and     _____

*3 marks*

**4** Work out the value of $7^2$.

$\boxed{\phantom{xxxx}}$

*1 mark*

**5** Find a number between 10 and 20 that is a multiple of 4 **and** a factor of 32.

$\boxed{\phantom{xxxx}}$

*2 marks*

# All Kinds of Numbers

**6** Which is larger: $5^2$ or $3^3$?

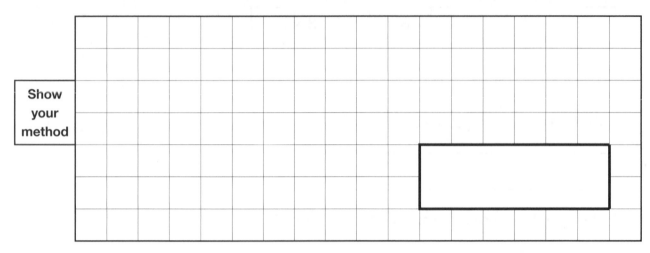

Show your method

2 marks

**7** Write down a number that you can divide by 2, 3 and 4.

2 marks

**8** Maisie has some counters.

She can arrange the counters into

| piles of 6 counters | or | piles of 15 counters | or | piles of 2 counters |

with none left over.

How many counters could she have?

2 marks

Total marks ............ /18

How am I doing?

10

# Addition and Subtraction

**1** This function machine adds 124 to every input number.

Write in the missing numbers.

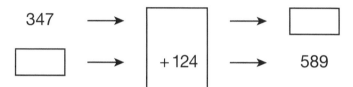

347 → +124 → □

1 mark

□ → +124 → 589

1 mark

□ → +124 → 406

1 mark

**2** Estimate the answer to 823 + 196 − 375.

Use your estimate to help you tick the correct answer.

□ 754          □ 644          □ 684

1 mark

**3** Farzia buys a loaf of bread for £1.34, a jar of jam for 85p, a bottle of milk for 49p and a packet of teabags for £2.89.

How much change does she get from £10?

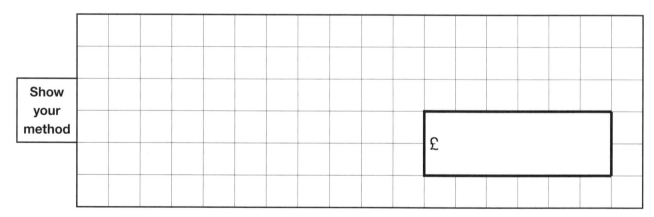

Show your method

£

2 marks

**4** Use this addition fact **1,371 + 2,463 = 3,834** to help you work out:

1,374 + 2,463 = □          1,375 + 2,465 = □

2 marks

# Addition and Subtraction

**5** The graph shows the numbers of passengers on four different trains one morning.

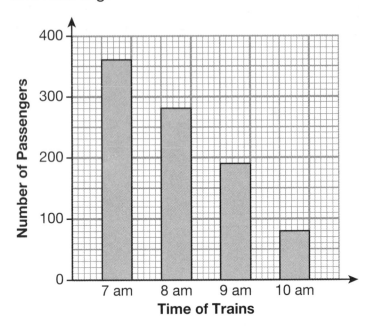

> Find the total number of passengers.

**6** A coach company has three coaches:

|  |  | Hire cost |
|---|---|---|
| **Coach A** | 52 passengers | £120 |
| **Coach B** | 30 passengers | £84 |
| **Coach C** | 44 passengers | £100 |

Miss Smith plans a school trip for 78 children and 6 teachers. She wants to pay the lowest possible hire cost.

> Which coaches does she need?

Show your working.

Coach [     ] and Coach [     ]

# Addition and Subtraction

**7** Write the missing numbers in this calculation:

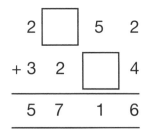

```
  2 [ ] 5   2
+ 3   2 [ ] 4
  5   7   1   6
```

1 mark

1 mark

**8** Circle two numbers that add up to 10,000 and have a difference of 2640.

| | | |
|---|---|---|
| 5,500 | 2,180 | 6,320 |
| 4,500 | 3,680 | 7,820 |

2 marks

**9** The table shows the number of phones a shop sells each month.

| Month | Number of phones sold |
|-------|-----------------------|
| Jan | 941 |
| Feb | 1,236 |
| Mar | 1,360 |

The shop's target is to sell 4,200 phones by April 30th.

How many more phones do they need to sell?

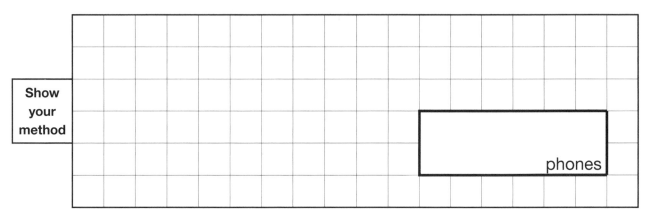

**Show your method**

phones

3 marks

13

# Addition and Subtraction

**10** Lucy buys furniture for her new house.

| Sofa £1,095 | TV £499 | Table £295 | Bed £795 | 4 chairs £190 |

She estimates the total cost like this:

1,100 + 500 + 300 + 800 + 200 = £2,900

**a)** Is her estimate more or less than the real cost?

Explain how you know.

_____

_____

2 marks

**b)** Lucy has £3,000 to spend. Will she have

☐ more than £100 left

or ☐ less than £100 left?

1 mark

**11** In June there were 12,460 visitors to a theme park.

In July the number of visitors increased by 9,862.

How many visitors were there in total in June and July?

Show your working.

[                    ]

3 marks

Total marks ............. /26          How am I doing?

# Short Multiplication

**1** Maria buys 10 of these pencils:

How much change does she get from £5?

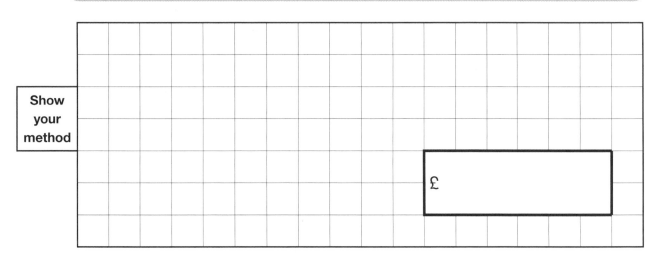

Show your method

£

2 marks

**2** There are 16 mugs in a box.

How many mugs are there in 8 boxes?

| | |
|---|---|
| | mugs |

1 mark

**3** Write in the missing numbers:

24.3 ⟶ × 10 ⟶ [ ]

1 mark

1.64 ⟶ × ____ ⟶ 1,640

1 mark

[ ] ⟶ × 100 ⟶ 135

1 mark

**4** Write in the missing numbers:

1 [ ] 7

×     5

6   8   [ ]

1 mark

1 mark

# Short Multiplication

**5** Silver balloons are sold in packs of 18. Blue balloons are sold in packs of 35.

Rio buys 2 packs of silver balloons and 3 packs of blue balloons.

How many balloons does he buy in total?

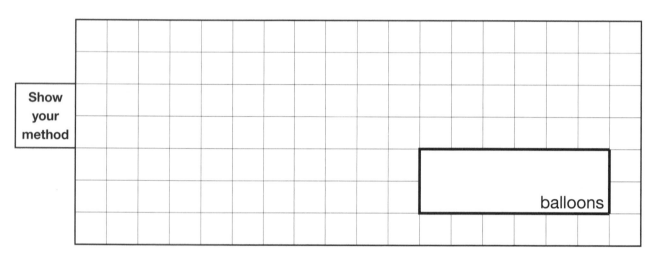

Show your method

balloons

*3 marks*

**6** Sara drives 32 miles to get to work every day.

She works Monday to Thursday every week.

How far does she drive from home to work and back every week?

[    ] miles

*2 marks*

**7** Use this multiplication fact **49 × 7 = 343** to work out:

50 × 7 = [    ]          49 × 8 = [    ]

*2 marks*

Total marks ............. /15          How am I doing?

# Long Multiplication

**1** There are 25 biros in a box.

How many biros are there in 18 boxes?

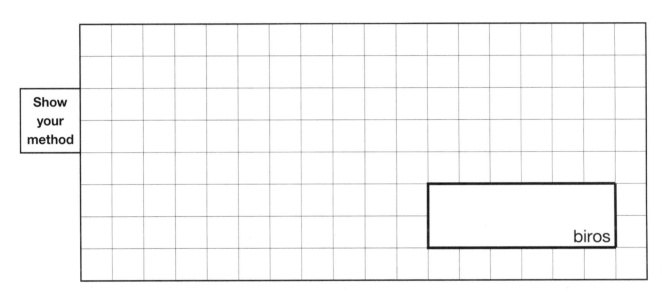

Show your method

biros

2 marks

**2** Work out $32^2$.

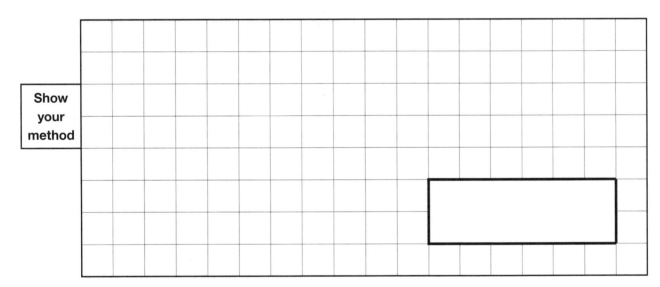

Show your method

2 marks

Total marks ............. /4          How am I doing?

# Short Division

**1** A box contains 6 eggs.

405 eggs need to be packed into boxes.

What is the smallest number of boxes you need to pack **all** the eggs?

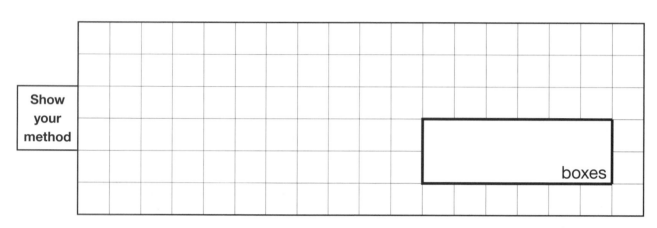

boxes

2 marks

**2** 4 friends share 69 marbles equally.

How many marbles are left over?

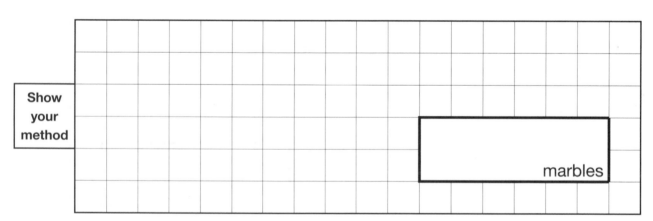

marbles

2 marks

**3** Write in the missing number.

$$7 \overline{)9 \boxed{\phantom{0}} 4}$$

with quotient 1 3 2 above

1 mark

# Short Division

**4** Work out:

28 × 3 ÷ 7

| Show your method | | | | | | | | | | | | | | | |
|---|---|---|---|---|---|---|---|---|---|---|---|---|---|---|---|

2 marks

**5** 6 people share this bill equally:

| 3 pizzas £26.85 | 6 desserts £23.55 |
|---|---|

How much does each person pay?

| Show your method | | | | | | | | | | | | | | |
|---|---|---|---|---|---|---|---|---|---|---|---|---|---|---|

£

2 marks

**6** 4 kg of bananas cost £3.48.

How much do 3 kg of bananas cost?

£

2 marks

Total marks ............ /11      How am I doing?

19

# Long Division

**1** There are 22 biscuits in a packet.

How many packets can you fill with 340 biscuits?

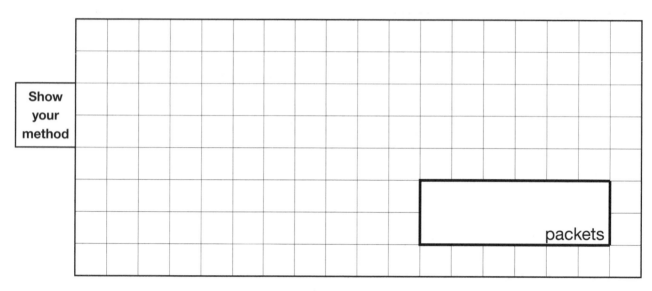

Show your method

packets

2 marks

**2** 15 kg of potatoes cost £19.20.

What do 4 kg of these potatoes cost?

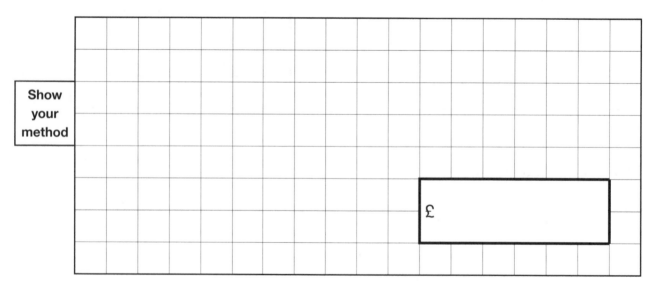

Show your method

£

2 marks

**3** Jon has 76 stickers. Bella has 16 stickers.

Tick the correct statement:

Jon has ☐ $4\frac{1}{4}$ times ⎤

☐ $4\frac{1}{2}$ times ⎬ the number of stickers that Bella has.

☐ $4\frac{3}{4}$ times ⎦

1 mark

**4** A snail moves 1 metre in 1 hour.

How far does it move on average in 1 minute?

Give your answer to the nearest centimetre.

| Show your method | | | | | | | | | | | |
|---|---|---|---|---|---|---|---|---|---|---|---|

cm

2 marks

**5** Use this division fact **448 ÷ 14 = 32** to help you work out:

448 ÷ 32 = ☐                    448 ÷ 7 = ☐

2 marks

Total marks ............. /9          How am I doing?

**1** Write the missing words and numbers.

428 has

☐ hundreds

1 mark

2 _____

1 mark

☐ ones

1 mark

**2** Here is a number written in Roman numerals.

**CXLIII**

Write the number in figures.

_____

2 marks

**3** Write these numbers in order, from largest to smallest:

59,000      251,200      32,481      17,420      170,315

☐        ☐        ☐        ☐        ☐

2 marks

**4** Circle the prime numbers in this box:

One is done for you.

| 1 | 15 | 2 | 8 | 13 | ③ | 9 |

2 marks

**5** You need 250 grams of flour to make 9 muffins.

Work out the amount of flour in 1 muffin, to the nearest gram.

Show your method

grams

2 marks

**6** Rob and Jo travelled around France and Spain by car.

At the start of their journey their car had done 52,215 km.

At the end of their journey their car had done 54,362 km.

Round the numbers to the nearest 100 to estimate how many km they travelled. Write the estimate.

km

2 marks

**7** 17 postcards cost £5.10.

How much does 1 postcard cost?

p

1 mark

Total marks ............ /14          How am I doing?

23

# Fractions and Decimals

**1**    **a)** Shade $\frac{1}{5}$ of this shape:

1 mark

**b)** Shade $\frac{2}{3}$ of this shape:

1 mark

**2**    Tick the calculation that has the smallest answer.

☐ $\frac{1}{4}$ of 20          or          ☐ $\frac{1}{3}$ of 18

Explain how you know.

_____

2 marks

**3**    Pia has 20 apples.

$\frac{3}{4}$ of her apples are red.

How many red apples does Pia have?

1 mark

**4**    Tom and Ben share a bar of chocolate.

Tom has $\frac{1}{8}$          Ben has $\frac{3}{8}$

What fraction of the bar is left?

1 mark

# Fractions and Decimals

**5** Jenny spends $\frac{1}{2}$ hour on her reading and $\frac{3}{4}$ hour on her maths homework.

How many hours does she spend studying in total?

| hours |
| --- |

1 mark

**6**

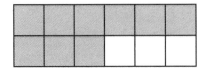

Complete these fractions to show how much of the grid is shaded:

$$\frac{\Box}{12} = \frac{3}{\Box}$$

2 marks

**7** Write <, > or = between each pair of fractions.

$\frac{5}{7}$ ☐ $\frac{10}{14}$          $\frac{3}{8}$ ☐ $\frac{10}{24}$          $\frac{2}{5}$ ☐ $\frac{12}{25}$

3 marks

**8** In an addition wall, you add the two numbers below to get the number above, like this:

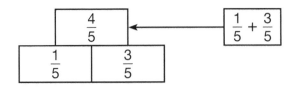

Complete this addition wall:

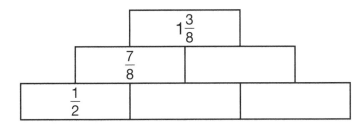

3 marks

25

# Fractions and Decimals

**9**    Write these fractions in order, starting with the smallest:

$1\frac{1}{4}$      $\frac{1}{3}$      $\frac{5}{6}$      $\frac{1}{8}$      $\frac{2}{3}$      $1\frac{1}{3}$

_____    _____    _____    _____    _____    _____

_3 marks_

**10**    Luke has £5 and spends $\frac{3}{10}$ of it on sweets.

Emily has £4.25 and spends $\frac{2}{5}$ of it on sweets.

Who spends more on sweets?

☐ Luke        ☐ Emily

**Show your method**

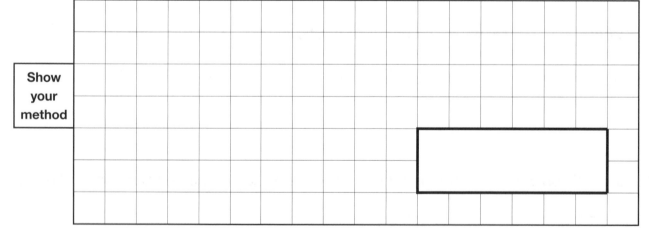

_2 marks_

**11**    Fill in the missing numbers:

$\frac{2}{3} \times \frac{1}{5} = \frac{2}{\Box}$          $\frac{1}{6} \times \frac{\Box}{\Box} = \frac{3}{12}$

_3 marks_

Total marks ............. /23        How am I doing?

# Decimals

**1** Circle all the numbers that have 7 tenths.

| 7.47 | 7.67 | 7.71 | 7.07 | 7.76 | 7.77 |

2 marks

**2** Circle the decimal that **does not** round to 7 to the nearest whole number.

| 6.7 | 7.4 | 6.8 | 7.5 | 6.92 | 7.19 |

1 mark

**3** Here are the 100 m race times for four runners:

| Runner | Time |
|--------|--------|
| Tom | 12.92 |
| Jim | 12.175 |
| Ben | 12.46 |
| Sam | 12.8 |

Who came    1st         2nd         3rd         4th?

3 marks

**4** Milly buys 5 ice creams for £1.79 each.

How much change does she get from £10?

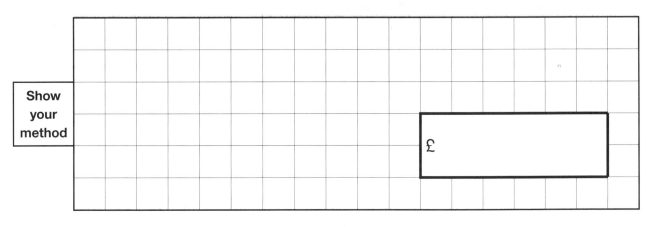

Show your method

£

2 marks

# Decimals

**5** Fay cuts a piece of wood 2.4 m long into 10 equal pieces.

How long is each piece, in centimetres?

cm

1 mark

**6** This formula converts metres to kilometres:

number of kilometres = number of metres ÷ 1,000

**a)** How many kilometres is 3,427 metres?       km

1 mark

**b)** How many metres is 3.54 kilometres?       m

1 mark

**7** Write <, > or = between each pair:

0.6       $\frac{5}{8}$

1 mark

0.84       $\frac{42}{50}$

1 mark

0.35       $\frac{1}{3}$

1 mark

**8** Can you share £10 equally between 9 people?

Yes         No

Show working to explain.

2 marks

Total marks ............ /16        How am I doing?

28

| Question | Answer | Maximum Marks |
|---|---|---|
| Pages 4–5 Place Value and Rounding |||
| 1 | Six hundred and nine | 1 |
| 2 | 8,950, 8,900, 9,000 | 3 |
| 3 | 76,521, 12,567 | 2 |
| 4 | 6,932, 7,032, 7,132 | 3 |
| 5 | 15,415 and 14,826 | 2 |
| 6 | 7 hundred thousand or 700,000 | 1 |
| 7 | 3) Madrid 4) Athens 5) Paris (2 marks for all 3 correct, award 1 mark if 1 error) | 2 |
| 8 | 2,432,511, 2,532,511 | 2 |
| Pages 6–7 Negative Numbers |||
| 1 | –2, –3, –4 | 3 |
| 2 | 6, 2, 1, 0, –2, –5 (3 marks for all correct, 2 marks for 4 or 5 correct, 1 mark for 2 or 3 correct) | 3 |
| 3 | **a)** Aberdeen **b)** Cardiff | 2 |
| 4 | –2°C | 1 |
| 5 | **–7**, –4, –1, **2, 5** | 3 |
| 6 | 8°C | 1 |
| 7 | **a)** Moscow **b)** Toronto | 2 |
| Page 8 Roman Numerals |||
| 1 | 24 | 1 |
| 2 | 10 minutes past 4 | 1 |
| 3 | **a)** MMIX should be ticked. **b)** MDCCIV, MCMLV, MMIV, MMIX, MMLIX (2 marks for all in the correct order, written as Roman mumerals; 1 mark for 3 or more correct or for: 1704, 1955, 2004, 2009, 2059) | 3 |
| Pages 9–10 All Kinds of Numbers |||
| 1 | $1 \times$ **12, 2** $\times$ 6, 3 $\times$ **4** | 3 |
| 2 | **a)** 1, 2, 4, 5, 10, 20 (2 marks for all six, 1 mark for five) **b)** 2, 5 (NB 1 is *not* a prime number) | 3 |
| 3 | Factors of 6: 1, 2, 3, 6; 1 + 2 + 3 = 6, (1 mark for all correct factors, 1 mark for 1 + 2 + 3, 1 mark for = 6) | 3 |
| 4 | 49 | 1 |
| 5 | 16 (award 1 mark for a multiple of 4, i.e. 12 or 20) | 2 |
| 6 | $3^3$ (award 1 mark for $3^3$ = 27 and / or $5^2$ = 25 shown) | 2 |
| 7 | 12, or a multiple of 12 (award 1 mark for a number divisible by two of 2, 3 and 4, e.g. 6) | 2 |
| 8 | 30, or a multiple of 30 (award 1 mark for a multiple of two of the numbers 6, 15, or 20, e.g. 12) | 2 |

| Question | Answer | Maximum Marks |
|---|---|---|
| | **Pages 11–14 Addition and Subtraction** | |
| 1 | 471, 465, 282 | 3 |
| 2 | 644 should be ticked. | 1 |
| 3 | £4.43 (award 1 mark for correct addition / subtraction methods shown, but with 1 error or incorrect final answer) | 2 |
| 4 | 3,837, 3,840 | 2 |
| 5 | 360 + 280 + 190 + 80 = 910 (award 1 mark for correct method but with 1 error) | 2 |
| 6 | Coach A and Coach C (2 marks for coaches correct, 1 mark for 78 + 6 = 84 **or** 52 + 30 = 82 **or** 52 + 44 = 96) | 3 |
| 7 | 2,**4**52 and 3,2**6**4 | 2 |
| 8 | 3,680 and 6,320 (award 1 mark for a pair that just add up to 10,000: 5,500 + 4,500 or 2,180 + 7,820) | 2 |
| 9 | 663 (1 mark for correct answer, 1 mark for 941 + 1236 + 1360 and 1 mark for 3537) | 3 |
| 10 | **a)** More, because all estimates > true price **b)** More than £100 left | 3 |
| 11 | 34,782 (1 mark for correct answer, 1 mark for 12,460 + 9,862, 1 mark for 12,460 + 9,862 + 12,460) | 3 |
| | **Pages 15–16 Short Multiplication** | |
| 1 | £1.40 (1 mark for correct answer, 1 mark for correct method. Award 1 mark for answer of £3.60 or 360p) | 2 |
| 2 | 128 | 1 |
| 3 | 243, × 1000, 1.35 | 3 |
| 4 | **137** × 5 = 68**5** | 2 |
| 5 | 141 (1 mark for correct answer, 2 × 18 = 36, 1 mark for 3 × 35 = 105) | 3 |
| 6 | 256 miles (1 mark for correct answer, 1 mark for 4 × 32 = 128 **or** 32 × 2 = 64) | 2 |
| 7 | 50 × 7 = 343 + 7 = 350      49 × 8 = 343 + 49 = 392 | 2 |
| | **Page 17 Long Multiplication** | |
| 1 | 450 (1 mark for correct answer, 1 mark for 18 × 25) | 2 |
| 2 | 1,024 (1 mark for correct answer, 1 mark for 32 × 32) | 2 |
| | **Pages 18–19 Short Division** | |
| 1 | 68 (1 mark for correct answer, 1 mark for correct method. Award 1 mark for answer of 67, **or** 405 ÷ 6 = 67.5) | 2 |
| 2 | 1 (1 mark for correct answer, 1 mark for $4\overline{)6^{1}9}$ giving $\frac{17}{2}$) | 2 |
| 3 | 9**2**4 | 1 |
| 4 | 12 (1 mark for correct answer, 1 mark for 28 × 3 = 84) | 2 |

| Question | Answer | Maximum Marks |
|---|---|---|
| 5 | £8.40 (1 mark for correct answer, 1 mark for correct method. Award 1 mark for answer of £50.40 **or** 8.4) | 2 |
| 6 | £2.61 (1 mark for correct answer, 1 mark for 3.48 ÷ 4 = 0.87 **or** attempt to multiply 0.75 × 3.48) | 2 |

### Pages 20–21 Long Division

| Question | Answer | Maximum Marks |
|---|---|---|
| 1 | 15 (1 mark for correct answer, 1 mark for correct method) | 2 |
| 2 | £5.12 (1 mark for correct answer, 1 mark for correct method) | 2 |
| 3 | 4¾ | 1 |
| 4 | 2 cm (1 mark for correct answer, 1 mark for correct method) | 2 |
| 5 | 14, 64 | 2 |

### Pages 22–23 Progress Test 1

| Question | Answer | Maximum Marks |
|---|---|---|
| 1 | **4** hundreds, **2 tens**, **8** ones | 3 |
| 2 | 143 (award 1 mark for 2 digits correct) | 2 |
| 3 | 251,200, 170,315, 59,000, 32,481, 17,420 (award 1 mark for more than 3 correct) | 2 |
| 4 | 2, 13 (NB 1 is *not* a prime number) | 2 |
| 5 | 27.7 ≈ 28 grams (1 mark for correct answer, 1 mark for $9\overline{)250}$) | 2 |
| 6 | 2200 km (award 1 mark for answer of 52,200 or 54,400) | 2 |
| 7 | 30p | 1 |

### Pages 24–27 Fractions and Decimals

| Question | Answer | Maximum Marks |
|---|---|---|
| 1 | **a)** 1 block shaded **b)** 4 blocks shaded | 2 |
| 2 | $\frac{1}{4}$ of 20 should be ticked. $\frac{1}{4}$ of 20 = 5 and $\frac{1}{3}$ of 18 = 6 (1 mark for correct answer; 1 mark for clear explanation) | 2 |
| 3 | 15 | 1 |
| 4 | $\frac{1}{2}$ (accept $\frac{4}{8}$) | 1 |
| 5 | $1\frac{1}{4}$ | 1 |
| 6 | $\frac{9}{12} = \frac{3}{4}$ | 2 |
| 7 | $\frac{5}{7} = \frac{10}{14}$, $\frac{3}{8} < \frac{10}{24}$, $\frac{2}{5} < \frac{12}{25}$ | 3 |
| 8 | (Also accept equivalent fractions) | 3 |
| 9 | $\frac{1}{8}$, $\frac{1}{3}$, $\frac{2}{3}$, $\frac{5}{6}$, $1\frac{1}{4}$, $1\frac{1}{3}$ (award 2 marks for 4 or 5 correct or for equivalent fraction in the correct order; award 1 mark for 2 or 3 correct) | 3 |

| Question | Answer | Maximum Marks |
|:---:|:---|:---:|
| 10 | Emily should be ticked. (1 mark for correct answer, 1 mark for £1.70 or £1.50) | 2 |
| 11 | $\frac{2}{3} \times \frac{1}{5} = \frac{2}{15}$, $\frac{1}{6} \times \frac{3}{2} = \frac{3}{12}$ | 3 |
| **Pages 27–28 Decimals** | | |
| 1 | 7.76, 7.77, 7.71 (award just 1 mark for 1 omission) | 2 |
| 2 | 7.5 | 1 |
| 3 | 1st Jim, 2nd Ben, 3rd Sam, 4th Tom (award 2 marks for 2 correct or 1 mark for 1 correct) | 3 |
| 4 | £1.05 (1 mark for correct answer, 1 mark for 5 × 1.79 = £8.95) | 2 |
| 5 | 24 cm | 1 |
| 6 | **a)** 3.427 km **b)** 3,540 m | 2 |
| 7 | $0.6 < \frac{5}{8}$, $0.84 = \frac{42}{50}$, $0.35 > \frac{1}{3}$ | 3 |
| 8 | No, because 10 ÷ 9 = 1.1111…. | 2 |
| **Pages 29–31 Percentages** | | |
| 1 | 15 | 1 |
| 2 | 72% | 1 |
| 3 | $\frac{3}{5}$, 0.4, $\frac{1}{4}$, 15%, $\frac{1}{10}$ (award 2 marks for 4 correct or 1 mark for 2 or 3 correct) | 3 |
| 4 | Set 1: 25%, $\frac{1}{4}$, **0.25**; Set 2: $\frac{3}{10}$, 0.3, **30%**; $\frac{1}{3}$ left over | 3 |
| 5 | 60% (1 mark for correct answer, 1 mark for $\frac{120}{200}$) | 2 |
| 6 | 253 ÷ 10 | 1 |
| 7 | Prices cut by $\frac{1}{4}$ | 1 |
| 8 | 10% off £89 should be ticked. 10% off £89 = £80.10, 25% off £110 = £82.50 | 3 |
| 9 | 20% of 42 = **8.4**; 5% of 42 = **2.1** | 2 |
| 10 | £3.00 | 1 |
| 11 | 7 | 1 |
| 12 | Most likely green; least likely orange | 2 |
| **Page 32 Converting Units** | | |
| 1 | 133 minutes | 1 |
| 2 | 1,000 | 1 |
| 3 | 5,400 cm, 1.36 km, 940 mm | 3 |
| 4 | 10 miles = 16 km, 2.5 miles = 4 km; 15 miles = 24 km | 3 |
| **Pages 33–34 Perimeter and Area** | | |
| 1 | B | 1 |
| 2 | 3 cm | 1 |

| Question | Answer | Maximum Marks |
|---|---|---|
| 3 | 22 cm (2 marks for correct answer, 1 mark for addition) | 2 |
| 4 | 18 cm², 9 cm² | 2 |
| 5 | A and C (1 mark for correct answer, 1 mark for A and C = 4 cm², 1 mark for B = 7.5 cm²) | 3 |
| **Page 35 3D Solids and Volume** | | |
| 1 | 5 cm³ | 1 |
| 2 | 1.75 litres (1 mark for correct answer, 1 mark for 7 × 250) | 2 |
| **Page 36 Money** | | |
| 1 | £177,745 (1 mark for correct answer, 1 mark for correct subtraction of any two numbers) | 2 |
| 2 | Deepak; 4 × £7.50 = £30; 5 × £5.80 = £29 | 3 |
| **Page 37 Time** | | |
| 1 | 7 | 1 |
| 2 | 42 minutes (1 mark for correct answer, 1 mark for correct method. Award 1 mark for answer of 10.45 or quarter to 11) | 2 |
| 3 | 12 minutes (1 mark for correct answer, 1 mark for identifying 9.53 and 10.05) | 2 |
| **Pages 38–39 Progress Test 2** | | |
| 1 | 211 | 1 |
| 2 | 3.49, 3.50, 3.51 | 3 |
| 3 | 10 inches, because 15 cm is about 6 inches | 1 |
| 4 | 24 cm (1 mark for correct answer, 1 mark for labeling 6 cm missing **or** showing addition with one length omitted.) | 2 |
| 5 | 53, 59 | 2 |
| 6 | Yes, £12 ÷ 5 = £2.40, **or** Yes, because you can divide £1 by 5, so you can divide £12 | 2 |
| 7 | **a)** 6°C **b)** 4 hours | 2 |
| 8 | Lisa £13.20, Mark £3.30 | 2 |
| **Pages 40–42 Angles** | | |
| 1 | (Tick only needs to be in one of the two places shown) | 2 |
| 2 | Parallel line: _____ Vertical line: | | 2 |
| 3 | | 2 |

| Question | Answer | Maximum Marks |
|---|---|---|
| 4 | line of symmetry — — — (Award 1 mark for one line correctly reflected) | 2 |
| 5 | A, C and D | 3 |
| 6 | 20°, 120°, 40°; 120° angle labelled O | 4 |
| 7 | 360° | 1 |
| 8 | 45° and 135°; 50°, 60° and 70° | 2 |
| 9 | *r* | 1 |
| 10 | **a)** 115° **b)** 50° | 2 |
| 11 | No, 2 obtuse angles > 180° | 2 |
| **Pages 43–44 Polygons** | | |
| 1 | 180° | 1 |
| 2 | 70° (1 mark for correct answer, 1 mark for 360 – 100 – 100 – 90 or equivalent) | 2 |
| 3 | 100°, 80°, 80° | 3 |
| 4 | 80° (1 mark for correct answer, 1 mark for 540 – 140 – 140 – 90 – 90 or equivalent) | 2 |
| 5 | 60° | 1 |
| **Page 45 Transformations** | | |
| 1 | | 2 |
| 2 | E is a translation, D is a reflection | 2 |
| **Pages 46–47 Topic 19 Statistical Representation and Interpretation** | | |
| 1 | Friday ⊠ ⊠ ▷  Sunday ⊠ ⊠ | 2 |
| 2 | Walk 12, cycle 3; 24 children in Class 5. | 3 |
| 3 | **a)** 6 **b)** 24 + 75 = £99 (1 mark for correct answer, 1 mark for correct method or award 1 mark for answer of £24 or £75) | 3 |

6

| Question | Answer | Maximum Marks |
|:---:|:---|:---:|
| | **Page 48 The Mean** | |
| 1 | $32 \div 4 = 8$ (1 mark for correct answer, 1 mark for 'their total' $\div$ 4) | 2 |
| 2 | Mean = $22 \div 6 = 3.666...$ kg, 3 weigh less than this (1 mark for correct answer, 1 mark for 'their total' $\div$ 6, 1 mark for correct answer for 'their mean') | 3 |
| | **Pages 49–50 Ratio and Proportion** | |
| 1 | Sue 30 cm, Jen 60 cm | 2 |
| 2 | 200 g, 50 g, 150 g | 3 |
| 3 | $\frac{1}{2}$ hour, 2 cars | 2 |
| 4 | 2%; Pritti, because 2% of £250 is only £5 (or equivalent) | 3 |
| 5 | 108 cm² (1 mark for correct answer, 1 mark for length of B = $6 \times 3 = 18$, 1 mark for 6 $\times$ 'their 18') | 3 |
| | **Pages 51–53 Algebra** | |
| 1 | $n + 6 = 10$ | 1 |
| 2 | £6; 16 (1 mark for correct answer, 1 mark for £4.80 $\div$ 0.30 (or 480 $\div$ 30)) | 3 |
| 3 | Any two of: 1 and 6, 2 and 5, 3 and 4 (in either order) | 2 |
| 4 | 6, 2, –2 | 3 |
| 5 | Any decimals $r$ and $s$ that add to 2, e.g. 0.5 + 1.5 or 1.2 and 0.8 | 2 |
| 6 | 10 | 1 |
| 7 | 192 m² | 1 |
| 8 | 7, 9.5, 12 | 3 |
| 9 | $2 \times 25 + 25 = 75$ mins = 1 hour 15 minutes; 6.35 pm (takes 125 mins) | 4 |
| 10 | $4950 \div 45 = 110$ m | 2 |
| | **Pages 54–56 Progress Test 3** | |
| 1 | | 1 |
| 2 | No $\quad 6 \times 24 = 144 < 160$ | 2 |
| 3 | $3000 + 6000 - 2000 = 7000$ | 2 |
| 4 | 9 tiles, 16 tiles | 2 |
| 5 | $\frac{1}{10}$, **0.1**, **10%**; $\frac{4}{10}$ or $\frac{2}{5}$, 0.4, **40%**; $\frac{3}{4}$ or $\frac{75}{100}$ **0.75**, 75% | 6 |
| 6 | 11°C | 1 |
| 7 | $5 \times n = 30$ or $5n = 30$, $n = 6$ | 2 |
| 8 | 5.2 km (1 mark for correct answer, 1 mark for 72.8 $\div$ 14) | 2 |
| 9 | $3 \times 2 \times 2 = 12$ | 2 |

# Progress Test Charts

## Progress Test 1

| Q | Topic | ✓ or ✗ | See Page |
|---|---|---|---|
| 1 | Place Value and Rounding | | 4 |
| 2 | Roman Numerals | | 8 |
| 3 | Place Value and Rounding | | 5 |
| 4 | All Kinds of Numbers | | 9 |
| 5 | Short Division | | 18 |
| 6 | Addition and Subtraction | | 11 |
| 7 | Long Division | | 20 |

## Progress Test 2

| Q | Topic | ✓ or ✗ | See Page |
|---|---|---|---|
| 1 | Addition and Subtraction | | 11 |
| 2 | Decimals | | 27 |
| 3 | Converting Units | | 32 |
| 4 | Perimeter and Area | | 33 |
| 5 | All Kinds of Numbers | | 9 |
| 6 | Decimals | | 28 |
| 7 | Negative Numbers | | 6 |
| 8 | Money | | 36 |

## Progress Test 3

| Q | Topic | ✓ or ✗ | See Page |
|---|---|---|---|
| 1 | Angles | | 40 |
| 2 | Short Multiplication | | 15 |
| 3 | Addition and Subtraction | | 11 |
| 4 | All Kinds of Numbers | | 9 |
| 5 | Percentages | | 29 |
| 6 | Negative Numbers | | 7 |
| 7 | Algebra | | 51 |
| 8 | Long Division | | 20 |
| 9 | 3D Solids and Volume | | 35 |

What am I doing well in?

_____

_____

_____

What do I need to improve?

_____

_____

_____

# Percentages

**1** In a survey on jam, 15% of people chose 'strawberry'.

There were 100 people in the survey.

How many chose 'strawberry'?

1 mark

**2** 28% of the people at a cinema are 65 years old or over.

What percentage are under 65?

%

1 mark

**3** Write in order, from largest to smallest:

15%      0.4      $\frac{1}{4}$      $\frac{3}{5}$      $\frac{1}{10}$

_____   _____   _____   _____   _____

3 marks

**4** Sort these into 2 sets of equivalent values, with one left over:

| 0.3 | $\frac{1}{4}$ | 25% | $\frac{3}{10}$ | 0.25 | 30% | $\frac{1}{3}$ |

Set 1    25%

1 mark

Set 2          0.3

1 mark

 is left over.

1 mark

# Percentages

**5** There are 200 people at a football match.

120 of them are male.

What percentage are male?

[        %  ]

*2 marks*

**6** Meg wants to find 10% of 253.

Tick the calculation she should use.

☐ 253 ÷ 100     ☐ 253 ÷ 10     ☐ 253 × 10

*1 mark*

**7** Two shops have money-off sales.

Tick the one that cuts prices the most.

☐ Prices cut by $\frac{1}{4}$          ☐ 20% off all prices

*1 mark*

**8** Tick the cheapest phone.

10% off £89          25% off £110

Show working to explain.

*3 marks*

# Percentages

**9** Complete:

20% of 42 = [ ] ← 10% of 42 = 4.2 → 5% of 42 = [ ]  $\overline{\text{2 marks}}$

**10** Tick the correct answer.

20% of £14.99, rounded to the nearest penny, is:

[ ] £2.99       [ ] £3.00       [ ] £1.50    $\overline{\text{1 mark}}$

**11** A zoo had 35 penguins in 2015.

In 2016, the number of penguins increased by 20%.

How many more penguins were there in 2016?

[ ] 3.5          [ ] 6          [ ] 7    $\overline{\text{1 mark}}$

**12** In a tin of sweets,

20% are orange

$\frac{1}{4}$ are red

$\frac{3}{10}$ are green.

Mary picks a sweet without looking.

Which colour is she     most likely to pick? _____    $\overline{\text{1 mark}}$

least likely to pick? _____    $\overline{\text{1 mark}}$

Total marks ............ /21        How am I doing?

# Converting Units

**1** What is 2 hours 13 minutes in minutes?

| minutes |
| --- |

1 mark

**2** The formula to convert grams to kilograms is:

| number of grams = number of kilograms ÷ 1,000 |
| --- |

How many grams are there in 1 kilogram?

1 mark

**3** Write the correct units.

| cm | | km | | mm |
| --- | --- | --- | --- | --- |

54 m = 5,400 ☐

1,360 m = 1.36 ☐

94 cm = 940 ☐

3 marks

**4** Complete these conversions:

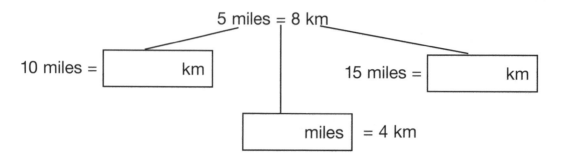

5 miles = 8 km

10 miles = ☐ km

15 miles = ☐ km

☐ miles = 4 km

3 marks

Total marks ............. /8      How am I doing?

# Perimeter and Area

**1** Here are three shapes:

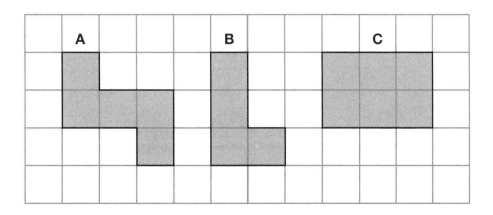

> Which shape has the smallest area?

[    ]

**2** This rectangle has a perimeter of 18 cm.

> Write in the missing length.

[    ] cm

6 cm

**3** Work out the perimeter of this shape:

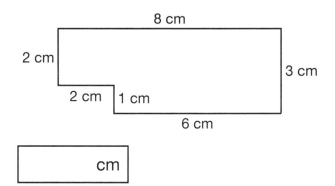

8 cm

2 cm

2 cm  1 cm

3 cm

6 cm

[        ] cm

# Perimeter and Area

**4** This parallelogram is divided into 2 identical triangles.

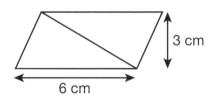

| Calculate: |

the area of the parallelogram [ cm² ]

1 mark

the area of one triangle [ cm² ]

1 mark

**5** Which two triangles have the same area?

[ ] and [ ]

Show your working.

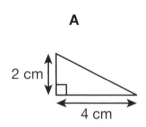

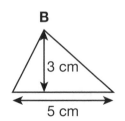

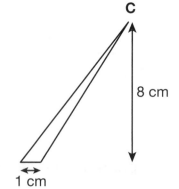

3 marks

Total marks ............ /9         How am I doing?

# 3D Solids and Volume

**1** This shape is made from 1 cm³ cubes.

Find its volume.

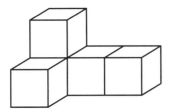

| cm³ |

**2** This jug holds 250 ml of water. 7 jugs of water fill this bucket.

What is the capacity of the bucket in litres?

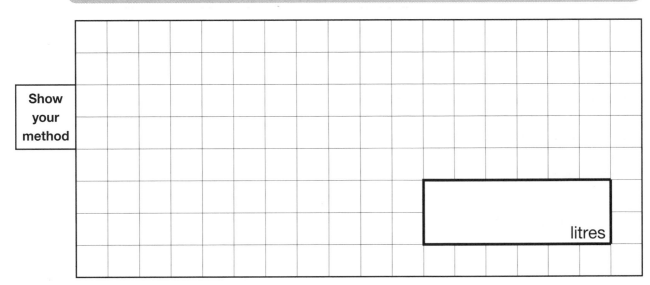

**Show your method**

litres

2 marks

Total marks ............. /3     How am I doing?

# Money

**1** The table shows the prices of 4 houses.

| House | Price |
|-------|-------|
| A | £165,250 |
| B | £247,300 |
| C | £342,995 |
| D | £294,500 |

What is the difference between the highest and lowest price?

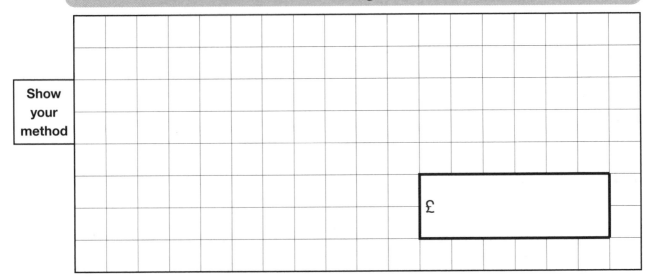

Show
your
method

£

2 marks

**2** Deepak works 4 hours for £7.50 an hour.

Jess works 5 hours for £5.80 an hour.

Who earns most?

Show working to explain.

_____

3 marks

Total marks ............ /5     How am I doing?

**1** How many months have 31 days?

```
[          ]
```

1 mark

**2** Debbie leaves home at:

She arrives at work at:

How long does it take her to get to work?

```
[          ] minutes
```

2 marks

**3** Here is a bus timetable.

| | |
|---|---|
| Smith Square | 9.48 |
| Johnson St | 9.53 |
| Walker Road | 10.02 |
| High St | 10.05 |

How long does the bus take to get from Johnson Street to High Street?

```
[          ] minutes
```

2 marks

Total marks ............. /5      How am I doing?

# Progress Test 2

**1** In a game, Tim scores 128 at level 1 and 83 points at level 2.

How many points does he score in total?

[ ]

1 mark

**2** Write the next three terms in this sequence:

3.46,    3.47,    3.48,    [ ] ,    [ ] ,    [ ]

3 marks

**3** Which is longer?

[ ] 15 cm    or    [ ] 10 inches

Explain how you know.

_____

1 mark

**4** Find the perimeter:

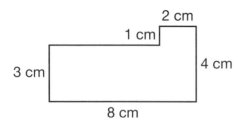

Perimeter = [        ] cm

2 marks

**5** Circle the prime numbers in this list:

50,   51,   52,   53,   54,   55,   56,   57,   58,   59

2 marks

38

**6** Can you share £12 equally between 5 people?

☐ Yes

☐ No

Show working to explain.

2 marks

**7** The graph shows the temperature in the playground one day.

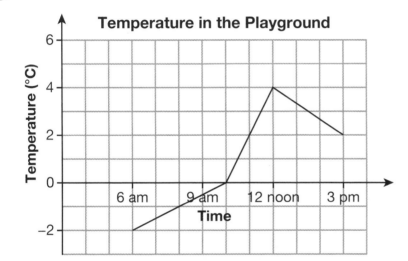

**a)** How much did the temperature rise between 6 am and 12 noon? _____  1 mark

**b)** For how long was the temperature below 0°C? _____  1 mark

**8** Lisa has 4 times more money than Mark.

Which of these amounts do they have?

| £3.30 | £6.50 | £2.50 | £12.60 | £13.20 | £7.30 |

Lisa ☐          Mark ☐

2 marks

Total marks ............. /15          How am I doing?

# Angles

**1** Put a ✓ by a right angle.

Put a ✗ by an angle smaller than a right angle.

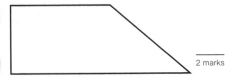

2 marks

**2** Draw a line parallel to this one:

_____

Draw a vertical line.

2 marks

**3** Here are the angles of a triangle.

| 100° | | 60° | | 20° |

Write them next to the correct angles in this triangle:

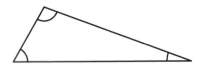

2 marks

**4** Complete the shape:

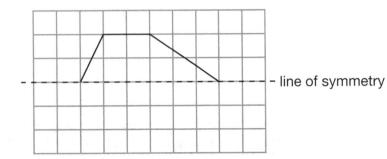

line of symmetry

2 marks

40

**5** Tick the isosceles triangles.

**A**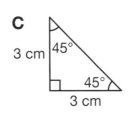

4 cm    4 cm

3 cm

☐

**B**

5 cm

7 cm

6 cm

☐

**C**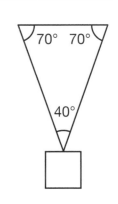

3 cm    45°

45°

3 cm

☐

**D**

70°  70°

40°

☐

_____
3 marks

**6** Measure the angles and write them in this triangle:

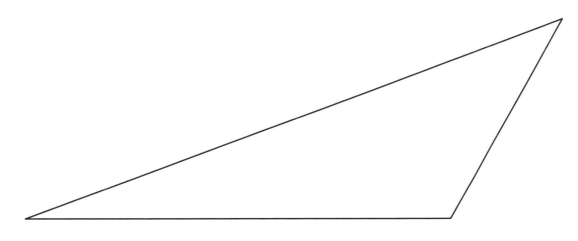

Mark the obtuse angle O.

_____
4 marks

**7** What do angles *a*, *b* and *c* add up to?

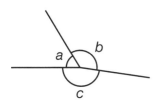

*a*    *b*

*c*

°

_____
1 mark

# Angles

**8** Tick the sets of angles that make a straight line.

☐ 45° and 135°

☐ 110° and 60°

☐ 50°, 60° and 70°

☐ 115° and 75°

*2 marks*

**9** Tick the angle that is vertically opposite to *p*.

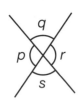

 *q*     *r*    ☐ *s*

*1 mark*

**10** Find the missing angles.

**a)**

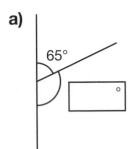

**b)**

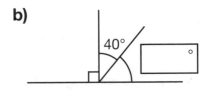

*2 marks*

**11** Can a triangle have two obtuse angles?

☐ Yes         ☐ No

Explain how you know.

_____

*2 marks*

Total marks ............ /23         How am I doing?

42

# Polygons

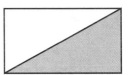

**1** The triangle is half the rectangle.

What do the angles in a triangle add up to?

|     |
|  °  |

1 mark

**2** Find the missing angle in this quadrilateral:

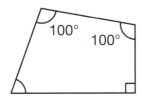

Show your method.     | ° |

2 marks

**3** This quadrilateral has one line of symmetry.

line of symmetry

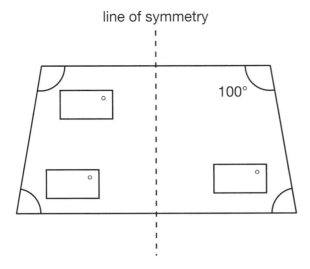

Find the missing angles.

3 marks

# Polygons

**4** The angles in a pentagon add up to 540°.

Find the missing angle in this pentagon:

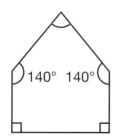

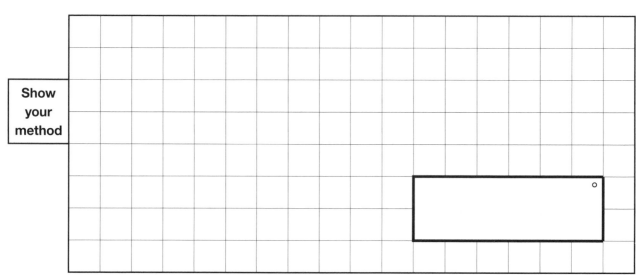

Show your method

2 marks

**5** This hexagon is made from 6 identical triangles.

Find the size of angle a.

1 mark

Total marks ............. /9          How am I doing?

44

# Transformations

**1**  **a)** Reflect shape A in the vertical mirror line. Label the new shape B.

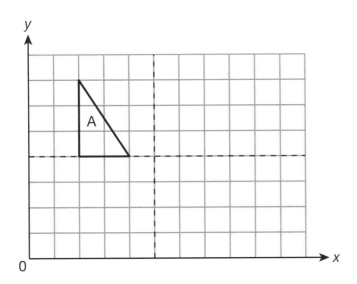

**b)** Reflect shape B in the horizontal mirror line. Label the new shape C.

2 marks

**2**

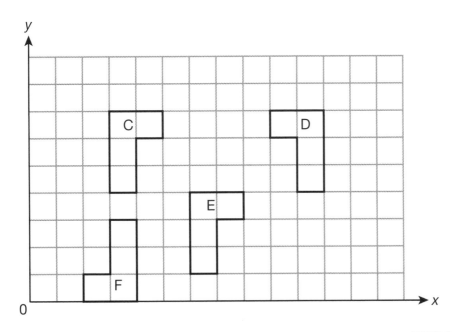

Which shape is:    a translation of shape C?

1 mark

a reflection of shape C?

1 mark

Total marks ............ /4          How am I doing?

# Statistical Representation and Interpretation

**1** The pictogram shows the number of emails Lola sends.

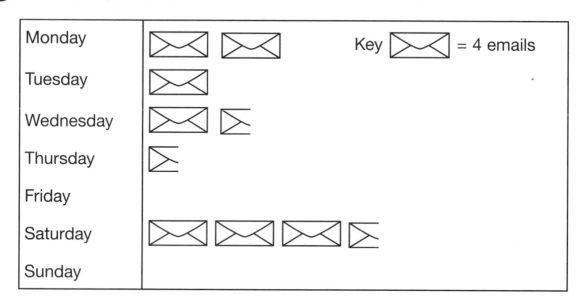

> Lola sends 10 emails on Friday. Add these to the pictogram.

1 mark

Lola sends 22 emails over the weekend.

> Complete the pictogram for Sunday.

1 mark

**2** The pie chart shows how the children in Class 5 travel to school.

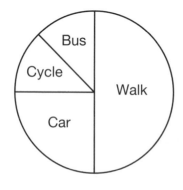

6 children travel by car.

How many children          walk? ☐          cycle? ☐

2 marks

How many children are in Class 5?          ☐

1 mark

**46**

# Statistical representation and interpretation

**3** The table shows the ages of children in a club.

| Age | Number of children |
|-----|---------------------|
| 7 | 12 |
| 8 | 8 |
| 9 | 11 |
| 10 | |

| Club Fees | |
|-----------|---|
| Under 8 | £2 a week |
| 8 or over | £3 a week |

**a)** There are 37 children in the club. How many children are aged 10?

1 mark

**b)** How much does the club get in fees each week?

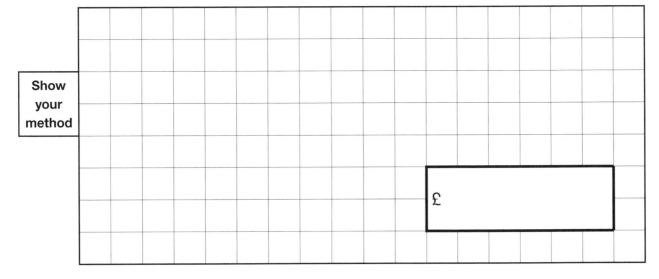

**Show your method**

£

2 marks

Total marks ............ /8     How am I doing?

47

Statistics, Ratio and Proportion

# The Mean

**1** Amy got these marks in four tests:

| Test | Mark |
|------|------|
| Test 1 | 8 |
| Test 2 | 5 |
| Test 3 | 9 |
| Test 4 | 10 |

What was her mean mark?

2 marks

**2** Here are the weights of six babies:

| Baby | Weight (kg) |
|------|-------------|
| Lily | 2.8 kg |
| Tom | 3.1 kg |
| Peggy | 3.4 kg |
| Ben | 4.7 kg |
| Josh | 3.9 kg |
| Molly | 4.1 kg |

How many babies weigh less than the average weight?

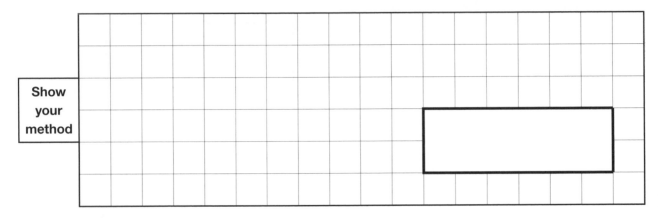

Show your method

3 marks

Total marks ............ /5          How am I doing?

48

# Ratio and Proportion

**1** Jen and Sue cut a 90 cm length of ribbon so that Jen's piece is twice as long as Sue's.

How long is:

Sue's piece? ☐ cm

*1 mark*

Jen's piece? ☐ cm

*1 mark*

**2** A recipe for 4 people uses 100 g of cheese.

How much cheese do you need for:

8 people? ☐ g

*1 mark*

2 people? ☐ g

*1 mark*

6 people? ☐ g

*1 mark*

**3** It takes 2 people $\frac{1}{4}$ hour to wash a car.

How long will it take 1 person?

☐ hour

*1 mark*

How many cars can 4 people wash in $\frac{1}{4}$ hour?

☐ cars

*1 mark*

# Ratio and Proportion

**4** Max had £100 in the bank. The bank paid him £2 interest.

What percentage is this?

[ ] %

1 mark

Pritti had £250 in the bank. The bank paid her £6.

Who had the higher rate of interest?

[ ] Max

[ ] Pritti

Explain how you know.

_____

2 marks

**5** These two rectangles are similar.

B   6 cm

A   2 cm

6 cm

Find the area of rectangle B.

Show your method

cm²

3 marks

Total marks ............ /13     How am I doing?

# Algebra

**1** I think of a number and add 6. My answer is 10.

> Write this using algebra. Use *n* for my number.

_____

1 mark

**2** Rose has a paper round.

> Use this formula to work out how much she gets paid for delivering 20 papers.

| pay = number of papers × 30 p |

£ [        ]

1 mark

One day Rose is paid £4.80.

> Use the formula to work out how many papers she delivered.

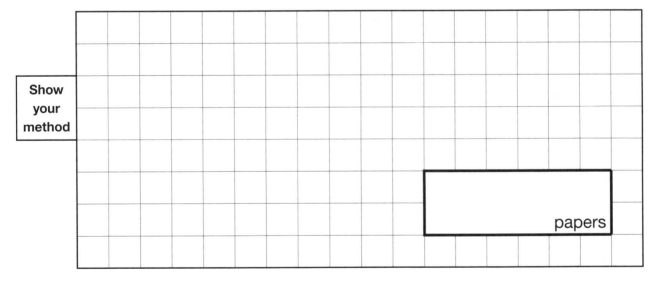

**Show your method**

papers

2 marks

51

# Algebra

**3**   $x$ and $y$ are whole numbers greater than 0.   $\boxed{x + y = 7}$

One pair of values for $x$ and $y$ is $\boxed{\phantom{xxx}}$ and $\boxed{\phantom{xxx}}$

1 mark

Another pair of values for $x$ and $y$ is $\boxed{\phantom{xxx}}$ and $\boxed{\phantom{xxx}}$

1 mark

**4**   The rule for this sequence is 'subtract 4 each time'

Write the next three terms:

10, $\boxed{\phantom{xxx}}$ , $\boxed{\phantom{xxx}}$ , $\boxed{\phantom{xxx}}$

3 marks

**5**   $r$ and $s$ are decimals.

Write two possible pairs of values so that:

$r + s = 2$

$r =$ $\boxed{\phantom{xxx}}$ and $s =$ $\boxed{\phantom{xxx}}$   or   $r =$ $\boxed{\phantom{xxx}}$ and $s =$ $\boxed{\phantom{xxx}}$

2 marks

**6**   Write the rule for this sequence:

2.63, 26.3, 263, 2630

Multiply by $\boxed{\phantom{xxx}}$ each time.

1 mark

**7**   The formula for the area of a rectangle is:

$\boxed{\text{area} = \text{length} \times \text{width}}$

A tennis court is a rectangle 24 m by 8 m.

Find its area.

$\boxed{\phantom{xxx} \text{m}^2}$

1 mark

**8** A sequence has first term 7 and rule 'add 2.5 each time'.

> Write the first three terms of the sequence.

☐ , ☐ , ☐

3 marks

**9** The time to cook chicken is given by this formula:

| Time = 25 minutes for each 500 g + 25 minutes |

> How long does it take to cook 1 kg of chicken?

☐ hour ☐ minutes

2 marks

> Dad puts a 2 kg chicken in the oven at 4.30 pm. When will it be cooked?

☐ pm

2 marks

**10** A football pitch is a rectangle 45 m wide. The area of the pitch is 4,950 m².

> Find the length of the pitch.

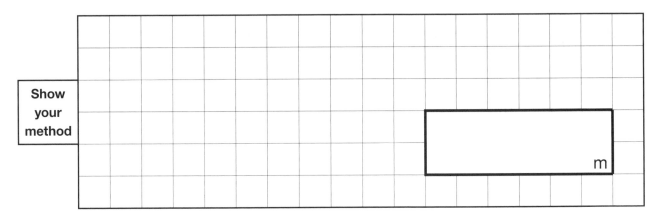

Show your method

m

2 marks

Total marks ............. /22     How am I doing?

# Progress Test 3

**1** Draw all the lines of symmetry on this rectangle:

**2** A school orders 6 sets of notebooks.

There are 24 notebooks in 1 set.

Are there enough notebooks for 160 pupils to have 1 each?

**Show your method**

 Yes          No

**3** Estimate the answer by rounding each number to the nearest 1000. Write the estimated answer.

2,593 + 6,215 – 1,800

**4** This set of 4 tiles can make a square.

Tick the sets of tiles that make a square.

☐ 8 tiles     ☐ 9 tiles     ☐ 12 tiles     ☐ 16 tiles

2 marks

**5** Complete the table:

| Fraction | Decimal | Percentage |
|----------|---------|------------|
| $\frac{1}{10}$ |  |  |
|  | 0.4 |  |
|  |  | 75% |

6 marks

**6** Work out the difference between the fridge temperature and the freezer temperature.

−8°C

3°C

☐ °C

1 mark

55

**7** Write this missing number problem using *n* for the unknown number.

$5 \times n = 30$ _____

Find *n*.　　　　$n = $ ☐

2 marks

**8** To train for a marathon, Seb ran 72.8 km in 14 days.

How many kilometres did he run each day, on average?

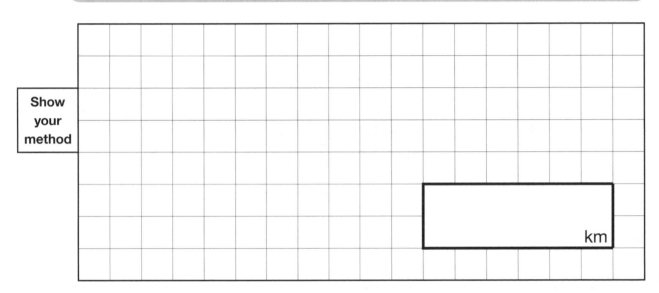

**Show your method**

km

2 marks

**9** How many 1 cm³ cubes do you need to make this cuboid?

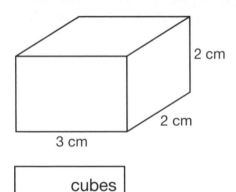

2 cm

2 cm

3 cm

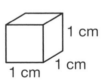

1 cm

1 cm

1 cm

☐ cubes

2 marks

Total marks ............../20　　　　How am I doing?